The French and Indian War:

Prelude to American Independence

Edited by Mary Alice Burke Robinson

Back-woodsman and Indian.
Both groups were expert at guerrilla warfare.
(La Gravure Francaise)

Discovery Enterprises, Ltd.
Carlisle, Massachusetts

ISBN 1-878668-82-X paperback edition
Library of Congress Catalog Card Number 96-86734

10 9 8 7 6 5 4 3 2 1

Printed in the United States of America

Subject Reference Guide:

The French and Indian War: Prelude to American Independence
edited by Mary Alice Burke Robinson

French and Indian War — U.S. History

Ticonderoga — U.S. History

Conquest of Quebec — Canadian History

Illustration/Photo Credits:

All art from *The French and Indian War - An Album,*
The Associates of the John Carter Brown Library,
Providence, Rhode Island: 1960,
except where otherwise noted in the text.

Cover art: Detail from "The Cruel Massacre of the Protestants, in North America Shewing how the French and Indians join together to scalp the English." London [c. 1760]

Table of Contents

Dedication

This book is dedicated to my parents, Alfred James Burke and Frances Goodnough Jenkins, whose love of reading and of learning was passed on to me very early in life, and has been a source of continuing satisfaction.

Introduction

by
Mary Alice Burke Robinson

Even today, after nearly 250 years, some historians disagree about the causes, dates, and even the name of the conflict that ended with Britain in control of North America.

Most often called the French and Indian War (referred to as the Seven Years War in Europe), its beginning dates may be given from as early as 1690, or 1713, 1744 or 1755. 1690 marked the beginning of a series of raids by Indians and French throughout New England, including the Deerfield massacre of 1704.

The Treaty of Utrecht, signed in 1713, ceded all of Nova Scotia (Acadia) and Newfoundland to Great Britain, including fishing rights. Other terms of the treaty were too vague to be workable and immediately caused problems which continued for fifty years.

The most significant event of the War of the Austrian Succession (called King George's War in the colonies) was the taking of Louisbourg on Cape Breton Island by an army raised by Governor Shirley of Massachusetts. Naturally the New Englanders were disgusted and disillusioned when the Treaty of Aix-la-Chapelle of 1748 gave Cape Breton Island back to the French, in trade for some lands in India.

In this book we will confine our study from 1755, when war was formally declared, to 1763, when the Treaty of Paris gave all the land east of the Mississippi —except Louisiana —to Britain. The dispute raged chiefly over Nova Scotia, Cape Breton, and northern New England, but extended much farther west because of fur trading rights, Native American involvement, and the French control of major waterways, which restricted English interests.

The French had made a powerful enemy when Samuel de Champlain killed some Iroquois braves with the first gun they had ever seen. Even after 100 years, the unfortunate Champlain incident was still very much alive in the minds of the Iroquois of the mid-eighteenth century, thus giving the British a powerful ally. Most other native tribes, however, sided with the French.

Many of the French were fur traders or missionaries, living with the Indians, learning their languages and customs. The British came to North America with their families. They wanted Indian land for farming and were less interested than the French were in learning about the native peoples, or in converting them to Christianity.

The French dominated the waterways by the mid-eighteenth century. By controlling the St. Lawrence River, they could reach the Great Lakes and the Mississippi River. The English were contained between the Atlantic coast and the Appalachian Mountain chain. They needed a water route so that they, too, could venture deeper inland to settle and to benefit from the rich fur trade. Many of the French and British claims overlapped, causing friction and open hostility.

One British route led up the Mohawk River to Oneida Lake, down the Oswego River to Lake Ontario. Another involved portaging from the Hudson River to Lake George, then to Lake Champlain, and down the Richelieu River to the St. Lawrence. The French were constantly challenging the British for control of these routes.

Little known, and less understood, the French and Indian War may well be considered a turning point in American history. The selections from original documents that follow will give the reader insights and views from a variety of people from different walks of life. (Their spelling and grammar have not been corrected.) Only a few realized the significance of the conflict which may properly be called a prelude and a training ground for another war that would impact the whole world. When the French and Indian War was officially over in 1763, the American Revolution was just thirteen years away.

Note: Words which appear in italics in sections of nonitalic text or in plain text in italic sections are defined in the Glossary on page 62.

Major Events of the Colonial Wars

1690 -1697 War of the Grand Alliance, King William's War in America.

1690 Indians and French raid Schenectady, New York, marking the beginning of a series of bloody raids in New York, New Hampshire, Connecticut, and Maine by both French and English colonists and Indians.

1701-1713 Queen Anne's War or War of the Spanish Succession; raids continue (the most famous one at Deerfield, Massachusetts in 1704).

1713 Treaty of Utrecht. French gave up claim to an area bordering Hudson Bay (rich in furs), Newfoundland, and Nova Scotia (Acadia).

1744-1748 War of the Austrian Succession in Europe, King George's War in America, Governor Shirley's War in New England.

1744 From the fortress at Louisbourg, Cape Breton Island, the French capture Canso, a fishing village in Nova Scotia. Indian raids resume.

1745 French abandon Louisbourg.

1748 Treaty of Aix-la-Chapelle, George II returned Louisbourg to the French in trade for some land in India, much to the disgust of New Englanders.

1754-1763 French and Indian War in North America, and the Seven Years' War in Europe (1756-1763).

1754 May 28. Col. George Washington attacked a French camp near Fort Duquesne, in the Ohio valley; built Fort Necessity.

July 4. He and his small group of Virginians were forced to surrender when his Indian allies left him.

French and British sent Regulars into the Ohio valley.

1755 July 9. Battle of the Wilderness (Braddock's Defeat).

General Edward Braddock and Regulars were surrounded; nearly 1000 killed or wounded; Braddock mortally wounded. His second in command, George Washington, organized a retreat.

The fighting spread; both sides began building up defenses.

Sir William Johnson built Fort Edward at the entry to The Carrying Place (a 15-mile *portage* about 50 miles north of Albany).

Fort William Henry on Lake George was built by British.

1755 French held Lake Champlain with a fort at Crown Point and built Fort Carillon (Ticonderoga) at southern end of Lake Champlain.

Robert Rogers organized his Rangers.

1756 French built Fort St. Frederick at Crown Point, New York.

1757 August 19. Fort William Henry Massacre. Fort captured by Montcalm.

Terms of Surrender included safe conduct for unarmed British soldiers, but about 150 were slaughtered before French officers could stop the Indians.

William Pitt, Prime Minister of Great Britain, intensified the war effort.

1758 July 8. French withstood British attack on Ft. Carillon. (See Peter Pond's account and the Ticonderoga legend in this book).

July 16. British gained control of Louisbourg, thus gaining control of the mouth of the St. Lawrence River.

November 25. British took Fort Duquesne, giving them control of the Ohio valley.

1759 May. Fort Niagara fell to British.

July 26. General Jeffrey Amherst took Fort Carillon, giving British control of Champlain valley. (See Rev. Henry True's account in this book.)

September 11. General James Wolfe defeated Marquis de Montcalm on the Plains of Abraham, Quebec. (See Nun's account in this book.)

October 12. French scuttled their fleet in Lake Champlain.

November. Rogers' Rangers make St. Francis Raid.

1760 August 25. British took Fort Levis, gaining control of the east end of Lake Ontario and the beginning of St. Lawrence River.

September 8. Montreal surrendered to British.

November. Robert Rogers sent by British to Detroit to accept French surrender.

By the end of 1760, French had surrendered almost all of its North American holdings.

1763 February 10. Treaty of Paris. French gave up all land east of the Mississippi River, except Louisiana.

Soldiers of the French and Indian War

Active participants in the French and Indian War were the Militia, Regulars, Rangers, Indians, and a few Swiss and German soldiers.

The Militia provided volunteers to serve in the provincial armies. They came from local communities and were made up of men who could be spared from farms and shops for short periods. They were ordinary civilians who were temporarily available to take up arms. The volunteers came mostly from farms. (Nine-tenths of the population at that time were living on non-commercial farms.)

By contrast, the Regulars were marginal members of society. They were from impoverished parts of Great Britain, and/or were convicts, social misfits, and poor men who had been made outcasts because of economic changes.

These two groups eyed each other with a mixture of disdain and respect. The Provincials admired the Regular soldiers' courage under fire, their teamwork and orderly ways, and the fact that they seemed able to stay healthier than the volunteers. Yet they were shocked at the regular soldiers' profanity and lack of regard for observing the Sabbath. They called the Regulars "Redcoats," "Bloodybacks," and "Lobster-backs." The Redcoats made fun of the Provincials, whom they considered country bumpkins. They were scornful of their spirit of freedom and independence.

Naturally this derision caused friction, often leading to fist fights and even riots. (Regular officers of both the French and British armies kept these groups apart as best they could, often teaming Provincials with Indians rather than with the Regulars.)

This rivalry extended to the officers. Provincial Army officers resented being made subordinate to British officers, who felt superior in training and social class, as they were often the younger sons of landed gentry. Most were unwilling to take advice from Provincial officers, while a few, such as young Lord George Augustus Howe, sent his soldiers to be trained by Rogers' Rangers in their ways of fighting. Lord Howe even went on expeditions with Rogers to

Above: Officer of the New York Militia Troop of Horse, 1725.

Right: Rural Militiaman from the 5th Worcester County Regiment, Massachusetts.

(Illustrated by Peter F. Copeland, Dover Publications, Inc.)

learn the Rangers' method "...of marching, ambushing, retreating, etc. and upon our return expressed his good opinion of us very generously."[1]

One particularly brave group was the Scottish highlanders. They suffered over 675 casualties in the unsuccessful attack on Fort Carillon (Ticonderoga). They were known to throw away their clumsy guns in favor of their favorite weapon, a broad sword. With one stroke they could slice off an arm or a head. Because they were fierce fighters and fought to the terrifying sound of skirling *bagpipes, they struck fear into the hearts of their enemies. And because they wore kilts, they were called "Ladies from Hell."*

Military Discipline

The Regular officers carried out a form of discipline considered extremely harsh by the Provincials. The object of severe punishment was to make the men feel that they had more to fear from their own leaders if they disobeyed orders than anything the enemy had to offer.

Sentences were swift, harsh, and carried out publicly — to serve as a deterrent to others. Officers had authority to pardon, and often did. Desertion, sleeping, or drinking while on sentry duty seem to be the most common infractions. The journal of Robert Webster, a private in a Connecticut regiment, mentions punishment for these crimes.

Source: "Robert Webster's Journal, Fourth Connecticut Regiment, Amherst's Campaign, April 5th to November 23rd, 1759," pp. 306-342, from *The Bulletin of the Fort Ticonderoga Museum*, Vol IX #5, Summer 1954.

"May the 29th. We marched over the west side of the city [Albany] and joined the regiment. There was one of the Rhode Island soldiers shot for desertion. We were drawn up and passed muster before the Regulars.

[1] *Journals of Major Robert Rogers*, New York, Corinth Books, 1961. Reprinted from the original edition of 1765, p 41.

Sabbath Day, 10th of June. This day there were two men brought to the pine tree to be whipped, one for leaving his post when on sentry and the other for getting drunk while on sentry but they were both forgiven.

Saturday, the 16th of June. This day John Williams of Colonel Fitch's Regiment in Captain Butler's Company was brought to the place where he was to be shot to death and there were twenty-four men to shoot him and the picquets of all the Provincial forces were brought up in front of Colonel Fitch's regiment and our regiment drawn up on the left of them. He was brought to the place where he was to suffer and made to kneel down and the platoon marched forth to shoot him but the General reprieved him. His crime was desertion.

The 13th of July. There was a Regular shot for desertion.

Friday the 3rd day of August. This day 100 men loaded *batteaux* with artillery stores and powder and shot and there was a regular hanged for deserting. He deserted to the French and Rogers' men brought him in yesterday with a French coat on him, and [he] was hanged immediately and his French coat was buried with him and a label on his breast.

Sabbath Day the 19th of August. Yesterday there were two men whipped, one for forging store orders. He was whipped eighty lashes."

The following are notes made by Sir William Johnson, an officer serving for the British. (See section on Johnson on pages 25-27.)

Source: *The Papers of Sir William Johnson*, prepared for publication by Milton W. Hamilton, Senior Historian, Division of Archives and History, Volume XIII, University of the State of New York, 1962, pp. 541-55.

"Prisr. [Prisoner] Ezekial Abbe private Man in Maj. Foots Compan accused of leaving his guard & being often call on to appear never came.

The Pris. pleaded Guilty of leaving his Guard but not guilty of never returning to it.

Evidence Capt. Harman

That he appeared at the Guard when at their first parading. That he was missing in half an hour after & did not return till abt. 2 hours before Sunset. Missed him again at 8 o Clock. When he had Liberty pass...he was again missing at the Alarm & at every time 'till after that time when relieving hours came.

That the Prisr. receive 10 lashes on his bare back at the head of each Reg. (Regiment) in Camp & his Crime published...."

Descriptions of other crimes and punishment followed. At the end of the letter, Johnson wrote:

"I approve the Sentence of the above Court Martial upon the several Criminals condemned to be punished & direct the Feild officer of the Day for to Morrow to see the Punishments & Sentenced duly Inflicted."

Camp at Lake George 23 Sept. 1755.
Wm. Johnson

This is part of a letter written in August 1759, to William Pitt, Prime Minister of Britain, in which Major-General Jeffrey Amherst describes the same event that Robert Webster did. See above.

Source: John Knox, *Historical Journal of the Campaigns in North America For the Years 1757, 1758, 1759,* and 1760, Major-General Jeffrey Amherst's Journal from July 27 to August 5, 1759. [Amherst to Pitt, August 5, 1759: Public Record Office, as before.], in Appendix, Part IV, p. 48.

"3rd (August 1759) a party I had sent to Crown point brought in a Deserter from late Forbes's in a french Coat, one that I had pardoned for desertion when I was at Fort George.

I thought it so necessary to make an immediate example that I had him hanged directly. sent two hundred Rangers through the Woods to Crown point."

Advertiſement.

DESERTED from Capt. *John Wright* of *Boſton*, on Wedneſday the 11th of this Inſtant, one *John Pepperrell*, (who was hired by ſaid *Wright* to go in the preſent Expedition) he is a Man about 40 Years of Age ; five Feet ſix Inches high, of a brown Complection, and wears his own dark, ſhort curl'd hair. Had on when he went away, a Cloth-colour'd Coat, ſtrip'd Breeches and Yarn Stockings.

Whoever will take up ſaid Deſerter, and bring him to the Sign of the Bear in *King-Street*, *Boſton*, or commit him to any Goal in this Province, ſhall have *Two Dollars* Reward, and all neceſſary Charges paid by me,

John Wright.

N. B. All Perſons are forbid harbouring, concealing or carrying of ſaid Deſerter, as they would avoid the Penalty of the Law.

Boſton, April 12th, 1759.

Advertisement for a Deserter

Sickness and Other Casualties

Often, more men died or were incapacitated by sickness, malnutrition, starvation, and accidents than by wounds. Robert Webster (op. cit., *p. 41) frequently speaks of illnesses such as measles, bloody flux, and smallpox.*

"Thursday the 21 of June. Two men died on the march with the heat.

Tuesday the 26 of June Joseph Ainsworth cut a man's leg almost off by accident and Abner Church was wounded by an accident.

Sabbath Day, the 7th of October. This day 94 sick men that belonged to our regiment were put on board the boat to go to Albany. Five of them belonged to Captain Holmes. Here are the names: Joseph Cotter, Luther Cady, James Franklin, Zebediah Chase, Peter Allard. Last night another died in our regiment. All the sick in all the Provincial forces were sent off 700 and six sick men went from this place. All provincials. Three men died in our regiment."

Although the Provincials were used to working under harsh conditions on their farms, they were more susceptible to disease while at war, because they were housed in close quarters with large groups of men. The Regulars had built up some immunities, and had become accustomed to meager diets of unwholesome food. More men were unfit to fight due to disease, starvation, and accidents than from wounds incurred in battles.

Robert Rogers and His Rangers

The Green Berets of the 18th Century

Robert Rogers was born on 18 November 1731 in northeastern Massachusetts and grew up in New Hampshire. He was only 11 years old when King George's War (1744) brought a series of violent and bloody Indian raids to a number of little settlements in New England. Well over six feet tall (unusual for that time), strong, intelligent, and resourceful, Rogers became very knowledgeable in the ways, customs, and lore of Indians.

Although he was valued by some British officers, and respected for his skill in scouting and guerilla warfare, the British never took his advice regarding fighting tactics. Even by today's standards, his manual contains effective techniques for those engaged in guerilla fighting. It has been said that if the British had learned and adapted techniques used by the Rangers, they might have won the American Revolution.

In his journal, Robert Rogers tells us of his expeditions as a scout, as the leader of men on raids, skirmishes, and campaigns. This uneducated backwoodsman uses a straightforward style and matter-of-fact approach that brings his adventures to life.

Rogers was often hampered by the ineptness of his commanding officers, even though he was eminently more qualified than they were to wage a successful campaign in the geographical locations where most of the fighting took place. Most British officers were rigid in their attitudes toward guerilla warfare in spite of their defeats and the success of the Rangers. The following excerpt from Robert Rogers' own journal is but one of many adventures carried out under appalling conditions. This reconnaisance was doomed by the stupidity of his commanding officer. Lieut. Col. Haviland let it be publicly known that Rogers was to lead 400 Rangers on a scouting expedition of French forts. Rogers suspected that the French had been informed of his plan and that he was walking into a trap.

Major Robert Rogers, Commander in Chief of the Indians in the Back Settlements of America. [London] 1776

Source: *Journals of Major Robert Rogers*, New York, Corinth Books, 1961. Reprinted from the original edition of 1765, pp. 58-64.

"March 10, 1758. I this day began a march from Fort Edward for the neighbourhood of Carillon, not with a party of 400 men as at first given out but of 180 men only, officers included....I acknowledge I entered upon this service and viewed this small detachment of brave men march out with no little concern and uneasiness of mind for as there was the greatest reason to suspect that the French were, by the prisoner and deserter above mentioned, full informed of the design of sending me out upon Putnam's return: what could I think! to see my party, instead of being strengthened and augmented, reduced to less than one half of the number at first proposed. I must confess it appeared to me (ignorant and unskilled as I then was in politics and the arts of war) incomprehensible; but my commander doubtless has his reasons and is able to vindicate his own conduct. We marched to the halfway brook in the road leading to Lake George and there encamped the first night.

The 11th we proceeded as far as the first Narrows on Lake George and encamped that evening on the east side of the lake; and after dark I sent a party three miles further down to see if the enemy might be coming towards our forts, but they returned without discovering any. We were however on our guard, and kept parties walking on the lake all night, besides sentries at all necessary places on the land.

The 12th we marched from our encampment at sunrise, and having distanced it about three miles, I saw a dog running across the lake whereupon I sent a detachment to reconnoitre the island, thinking the Indians might have laid in ambush there for us; but no such could be discovered; upon which I thought it expedient to put to shore, and lay by till night to prevent any party from descrying us on the lake, from hills or otherwise. We halted at a place called Sabbath Day Point on the west side of the lake, and sent out parties to look down the lake with perspective glasses which we had for that purpose. As soon as it was dark we proceeded down the lake. I sent Lieutenant Philips with fifteen men as an advanced guard some of whom went before him on skates while Ensign Ross flanked us on the left under the west shore, near which we kept the main body marching as close as possible to prevent separation, it being a very dark night. In this manner we continued our march till within eight miles of the French advanced guards, when Lieutenant Philips sent a man on skates back to me to desire me to halt; upon which I ordered my men to squat down upon the ice. Mr Philips soon came to me himself, leaving his party to look out, and said, he imagined he had discovered a fire[1] on the east shore but was not certain; upon which I sent with him Ensign White, to make further discovery. In about an hour they returned, fully persuaded that a party of the enemy was encamped there. I then called in the advanced guard and flanking party, and marched on to the west shore where in a thicket we hid our sleds and packs, leaving a small guard with them, and with the remainder I marched to attack the enemy's encampment, if there was any; but when we came near the place, no fires were to be seen, which make us conclude that we had mistaken some bleach patches of snow, or pieces of rotten wood, for fire (which in the night, at a distance, resembles it) whereupon we returned to our packs, and there lay the remainder of the night without fire.

The 13th, in the morning I deliberated with the officers how to proceed, who were unanimously of opinion that it was best to go by land in snowshoes lest the enemy should discover us on the lake; we accordingly continued our march on the west side, keeping on the back of the mountain that overlooked the French advance guards. At twelve of the clock we halted two miles west of those guards, and there refreshed ourselves till three, that the day-scout from the fort might be returned home before we advanced; intending at night to ambuscade some of their roads in order to entrap them in the morning. We then marched in two divisions, the one headed by Captain Bulkley, the other by myself: Ensigns White and Wait had the rear guard and the other officers were posted properly in each division, having a rivulet at a small dis-

[1] A small party of the French, as we have since heard, had a fire here at this time; but, discovering my advanced party, extinguished their fire, and carried the news of our approach to the French fort.

tance on our left and a steep mountain on our right. We kept close to the mountain that the advance guard might better observe the rivulet, on the ice of which I imagined they would travel if out, as the snow was four feet deep and very bad travelling on snowshoes. In this manner we marched a mile and a half, when our advanced guard informed me of the enemy being in their view; and soon after, that they had ascertained their number to be ninety-six, chiefly Indians. We immediately laid down our packs, and prepared for battle, supposing there to be the whole number or main body of the enemy, who were marching on our left up the rivulet upon the ice. I ordered Ensign M'Donald to the command of the advanced guard which, as we faced to the left, made a flanking party to our right. We marched to within a few yards of the bank which was higher than the ground we occupied; and observing the ground gradually to descend from the bank of the rivulet to the foot of the mountain, we extended our party along the bank far enough to command the whole of the enemy's at once; we waited till their front was nearly opposite to our left wing when I fired a gun as a signal for a general discharge upon them; whereupon we gave them the first fire which killed above forty Indians; the rest retreated and were pursued by about one half of our people. I now imagined the enemy totally defeated, and ordered Ensign M'Donald to head the flying remains of them that none might escape; but we soon found our mistake, and that the party we had attacked were only their advance guard, their main body coming up, consisting of 600 more, Canadians and Indians; upon which I ordered our people to their own ground, which we gained at the expense of fifty men killed; the remainder I rallied, and drew up in pretty good order, where they fought with such intrepidity and bravery as obliged the enemy (tho' seven to one in number) to retreat a second time; but we not being in a condition to pursue them, they rallied again, and recovered their ground, and warmly pushed us in front and both wings, while the mountain defended our rear; but they were so warmly received that their flanking parties soon retreated to their main body with considerable loss. This threw the whole again into disorder, and they retreated a third time; but our number being now too far reduced to take advantage of their disorder, they rallied again, and made a fresh attack upon us. About this time we discovered 200 Indians going up the mountain on our right, as we supposed, to get possession of the rising ground and attack our rear; to prevent which I sent Lieutenant Philips with eighteen men to gain the first possession and beat them back; which he did: and being suspicious that the enemy would go round on our left and take possession of the other part of the hill, I sent Lieutenant Crafton with fifteen men to prevent them there; and soon after desired two Gentlemen who were volunteers in the party, with a few men to go and support him, which they did with great bravery.

The enemy pushed us so close in front that the parties were not more than twenty yards asunder in general and sometimes intermixed with each other. The fire continued almost constant for an hour and a half from the beginning of the attack, in which time we lost eight officers and more than 100 private men killed on the spot. We were at last obliged to break, and I with about twenty men ran up the hill to Philips and Crafton where we flopped and fired on the Indians who were eagerly pushing us with numbers that we could not withstand. Lieutenant Philips being surrounded by 300 Indians, was at this time capitulating for himself and party on the other part of the hill. He spoke to me and said if the enemy would give them good quarters, he thought it best to surrender, otherwise that he would fight while he had one man left to fire a gun.[2]

I now thought it most prudent to retreat and bring off with me as many of my party as I possibly could, which I immediately did; the Indians closely pursuing us at the same time took several prisoners. We came to Lake George in the evening, where we found several wounded men whom we took with us to the place where we had left our sleds, from whence I sent an express to Fort Edward, desiring Mr. Haviland to send a party to meet us and assist in bringing in the wounded; with the remainder I tarried there the whole night, without

[2] This unfortunate officer and his whole party, after they surrendered upon the strongest assurances of good treatment from the enemy, were inhumanly tied up to trees and hewn to pieces in a most barbarous and shocking manner.

fire or blankets, and in the morning we proceeded up the lake, and met with Captain Stark at Hoop Island, six miles north from Fort William Henry, and encamped there that night; the next day being the 15th, in the evening, we arrived at Fort Edward.

The number of the enemy was about 700, 600 of which were Indians. By the best accounts we could get, we killed 150 of them and wounded as many more. I will not pretend to determine what we should have done had we been 400 or more strong; but this I am obliged to say of those brave men who attended me (most of whom are now no more) both officers and soldiers in their respective stations behaved with uncommon resolution and courage; nor do I know an instance during the whole action in which I can justly impeach the prudence or good conduct of any one of them."

Robert Rogers was brave, adventurous, responsible, and loyal to his men. History was not kind to him. Promises, made to him by the British regarding pay for himself and his men, and for provisions, were not kept, and he became destitute. He was even thrown into prison for debts incurred while recruiting and provisioning men as ordered by British commanders, who then never reimbursed him. It is unfortunate that he is not remembered for his description of his journey through the wilderness on the way to Detroit to accept the surrender of the French, or one of his other valiant exploits. Sadly, he is most remembered for the terrible raid on St. Francis, an Indian village. This raid was accomplished under direct orders of General Jeffrey Amherst in retaliation for the harsh raids these Canadian Indians had been making on settlements in northern New England.

What is not generally known is the disastrous return to Crown Point, which was only accomplished through the perseverance, ingenuity, and skill of Robert Rogers. He and his men endured unspeakable hardship, partly because of one lazy English officer. The formal report of the St. Francis expedition made to Gen. Amherst is fairly succinct, but Rogers gives a much fuller account in his journal.

The novel, Northwest Passage, *by Kenneth Roberts, is a fictionalized biography of Robert Rogers.*

Others Involved in the French and Indian War

Voyageurs

Most voyageurs took no active part in the war, but they often served as guides and interpreters, and had a vested interest in the war's outcome. One of the basic reasons for the French and Indian War was control of the water routes to the fur trading areas.

As a group, the voyageurs were strong, independent men who were used to primitive living. They lived with Indians, learned their languages and customs, and had traveled Indian routes to the interior long before explorers such as Lewis and Clark made their systematically recorded journey.

They usually left Montreal in May, traveling in large canoes that could carry several ninety-pound bales of goods to trade with the Indians for furs. They built small forts (stockades with a cabin or two inside), which the Indians and their families frequently visited.

It took a great deal of skill and awareness of native customs to deal successfully with the Indians. Fluency in one tribe's language might be of no value at all in speaking to those of a different tribe.

It was customary to give gifts freely as the trader went through one Indian tribe's land on his way to that of another. The route could be dangerous — depending on which tribes were at war or involved in a feud. If the voyageur had married a woman of a warring or feuding tribe, he would be barred from passing.

Following is an excerpt from Marie Sandoz. Not all beaver men were neutral as Marie Sandoz makes clear.

Source: Sandoz, Marie, *The Beaver Men: Spearheads of Empire*, Lincoln, Nebraska: Univ. of Nebraska Press, 1978, p. 142.

"Each summer from 1754 to the surrender of Canada war parties from as far west as the Missouri and the Plains went to join Charles Langlade, the mixed-blood trader of Green Bay, leading a breed and Indian force against the British. He was credited with planning the ambush of Braddock's troops, where over 900 were reported dead and wounded, including sixty-three of the eighty-nine officers, killed trying to rally the soldiers who were running away. Many more would have died if Langlade's Indians had not stopped to do a little scalping and jerking red coats off. Two years later they defeated a raiding party of Rogers' Rangers and many served in the Quebec campaign under Montcalm in 1759."

American Indians

The Indians were intensely independent. French and British officers who spent much time dealing with them found them to be very effective as scouts, guides, and raiders. But they had to be cajoled and given many presents before they would agree to go into battle. Even then, they might refuse if they did not like or respect their chief or the white officer. If the battle was not going well, they would fade off into the woods. In battle, they often would stop to take scalps rather than moving forward. Many prisoners begged for death rather than endure the horrible tortures that awaited them. Sometimes a prisoner would be adopted by a family who had lost a brave or a child. Children might be taken into a family or sold back to their own families.

In the Spring, prisoners were often taken to Montreal to be sold back to representatives of white communities. However, there are records of children who grew up in a tribe and refused to go back. One such was Eunice Williams of Deerfield, Massachusetts, who was captured by Abenakis of the St. Francis village. Williams' brother Stephen fought at Crown Point in 1755.

Sir William Johnson and the Indians

One of the great historical figures to emerge in the French and Indian War is Sir William Johnson of the Mohawk Valley in New York. Sir William was commissioned by King George II in 1753 to obtain the support of the Iroquois on the side of the British. He was successful in this because he was respected and trusted by the Indians. He called meetings with their chiefs often, and was able to obtain their commitment.

In 1756, he was made "Superintendent of Indian Affairs for the Northern District" and received a commission as "Colonel of the Six Nations" (the Iroquois). He himself led Militia and Indians into battle on more than one occasion. He was totally committed to Indian affairs, often traveling long distances to meet at council fires. The area around his own home was usually teeming with Indians, traders, merchants, army officers, travelers. He had built a handsome house which was part of a fortified garrison, protected by soldiers. A much grander house called Johnson Hall was built by Sir William in 1763, and is now open to visitors in Johnstown, New York.

French officers were very aware of the relationship between Johnson and the Iroquois as Louis de Bougainville stated over and over in his journals. Bougainville was aide-de-camp to Marquis de Montcalm during the French and Indian War and kept a journal throughout his stay in America. A brilliant and perceptive man, Bougainville was not popular with politicians because of his outspoken criticism of political situations in Europe and of graft and mismanagement during the war. In 1766, he led a scientific expedition around the world and explored the South Pacific, and during the American Revolution, he served under Admiral de Grasse in the French navy.

His published journals make fascinating reading, as he fought in many important battles and was entirely candid in his opinions. An excerpt follows.

Source: Bougainville, Louis Antoine de, comte, *Adventure in the Wilderness; the American Journals of Louis Antoine de Bougainville*, translated and edited by Edward P. Hamilton, 1st ed., Norman, University of Oklahoma, 1964, pp. 35, 246.

"Johnson concerns himself only with Indian affairs, he is the chief of that department. He has gathered together four or five hundred Indians from the regions of the Delaware, the Susquehanna, Seneca, etc., that we call Moraigans [Mohicans]. We do not know the destination of the Mohawks, to the number of one hundred, who have taken up the hatchet against us."

....

"Johnson has gone off again with all his Indians; a body of three thousand men and five six-pounders have followed him toward the Mohawk River."

Sir William Johnson was a devoted and loyal champion of the Indians. He was willing to persist in matters where they needed a prominent and respected person to represent them. Much of his time was spent attending to Indian affairs as his manuscripts show, meeting with the Indians, listening to their demands as they bargained with one another, trading wampum belts, and goods and supplies for warriors. He was accessible to them and maintained an almost paternalistic attitude toward the Indians who needed constant reassurance accompanied by tangible proof of promises made to them. They, in turn, trusted and respected him.

Source: Richard E. Day, Compiler, *Calendar of the Sir William Johnson Manuscripts in the New York State Library*, Albany, University of the State of New York, 1909, pp. 102-175.

"1760 April 8 Fort Johnson Sir William Johnson to Brig. Gen Gage, asking permission to feed Mohawks impoverished by destruction of their crops by droves of cattle passing through their fields, presenting their claim for damages, and asking for wagons and boats.

1760 April 13 Albany Thomas Gage, consenting to furnish wagons and boats; promising to order provisions to be issued to Mohawks at Forts Hunter and Hendrick and to refer claim to Gen Amherst....

1760 April 25 Fort Johnson Sir William Johnson to Gen Gage, pressing the matter of boats and wagons to carry Indian stores, denouncing deputy quartermasters who withhold them..."

"The Indians Giving a Talk to Colonel Bouquet in a Conference at the Council Fire." (From William Smith. An Historical Account of the Expedition against the Ohio Indians. London, 1776. (By Pennsylvania artist, Benjamin West.) This is typical of the council meetings held in 18th century America.

Civilians Caught in the War

The French and British took prisoners in order to get information about the enemy. The captives taken solely for this purpose were called "living letters" by the Rangers. A living letter was usually released after he had given information.

Civilians: French-Canadians

Most French-Canadians had very little knowledge or interest in the political situation between France and Britain. They wanted to remain neutral. It was their refusal to take an oath of allegiance to the king of Britain that culminated in the diaspora. *Longfellow's poem, "Evangeline," is the story of this tragic event. John Thomas, a surgeon from Massachusetts, was assigned to General Winslow's expedition to expel the Acadians in April, 1755. In his journal, Thomas matter-of-factly tells of the destruction and finally the dispersal of the Acadians. Note his apparent lack of regard for the people who were made refugees and fugitives by a situation which was none of their doing and in which they had very little interest.*

Source: "Diary of John Thomas, Surgeon," in *Winslow's Expedition of 1755 Against the Acadians*, uncatalogued, Special collections: CIHM 41402, pp. 10-13, Stauffer Library, Queen's University, Kingston, Ontario, Canada.

"August 25. 10 men returned upon Party that have been out with Capt willard to Cobigate &c and thay Brought in Several Prisoners Burnt Several Fine Viliges.

August 28. major Frye with a Party of 200 men Imbarked on Board Capt Cobb Newel & adam to Go to Sheperday & take what French thay Could & burn thare viliges thare & at Petcojack.

August 30. Cloudy uncomfortable wather Capt Gillbert Marched to the Bay of vert with a Party of 50 men to Bring in what Inhabitants he Could Find & Burn thare Vileges.

September 2. Plesant Day major Frye Sent Lieut Jne Indient on Shore with men to Burn a Vilige at a Place Called Petejack after thay had Burnt Several Houses & Barns, thay went about to Burn a New mass-house (church) a Large Number of French & Indians Ran upon them out of the Wood & Fired on them so thay ware obliged to Retreat Doct march who had Just Joyned him with 10 men from Capt Speakman's Party who Came on Shore the other Side of ye Vilige was Killed on the Spot 22 more Killed & taken Seven wounded Badly.

September 13. Raney Day we Continue Sending the Inhabitants on Board the Transport.

September 18. very Hard Gail of wind much Rain & Snow the Camp Greatly Torne to Peases with ye wind major rible Returned with his Party having Burnt 200 Houses & Barns.

October 9. Capt Rowse arived here from Hallefax In order to Hurrey ye Fleet with ye Prisoners from this Place.

October 11. Stormy Day Capt Dogget Sailed for Boston the Last Party of French Prisoners ware Sent on Board ye vesels In order to be Sent out of the Province.

October 13. Capt Rowse Sailed this morning with ye Fleet Consisting of 10 Sail under his comand thay Caryed Nine Hundred & Sixty French Prisoner: with them Bound to South Carolina.

November 15. Plesant Day we Burnt a Large mass house & 97 Houses more we met Capt Stevens with 200 men to Reinforse us we Returned to west Cook at Night whare we met Capt Hill with ye Regulars Colonel Scot major Prible & Several other officers with them & a No (number) of our Troops Came over to us In order to march with us to Memoramcook a vilege about 13 miles from West Cook.

November 17. Plesant Day we marched Last Night about 11 Clock with 700 men under Comand of Colonel Scot we marched all Night very Bad Traviling Came to memoramcook about Break of Day we Sorounded about 200 Houses but thay were all Deserted Except one house whare we Found 9 women & Children but no men ye most of them ware sick we Burned 30 Houses Brought away one woman 200 Head of Neat Cattle 20 Horses...."

The dispersal of these people was ordered on his own authority by the English Governor of Nova Scotia, Charles Lawrence. He exiled them with no preliminary planning, leaving it up to the captains of ships to decide where the prisoners should be taken. The governors of the colonies were not even informed. Without permission or advance warning, destitute French-speaking men, women, and children were almost literally dumped ashore. They were not welcomed or wanted. Georgia refused them, not even allowing them to land. Maryland, Pennsylvania, Massachusetts, and Connecticut were the kindest. One might think that South Carolina would have received them more cordially because it had a large French population. But South Carolina's Frenchmen were Hugenots (Protestants) and the Acadians were Roman Catholics. Consequently, they were not treated well in South Carolina.

A few went to Martinique in the West Indies. Many went to New Orleans where the word "Acadian" was corrupted to "Cajun." Years after the French and Indian War was over, many returned to Nova Scotia and took the oath of allegiance to the King of Britain.

Robert Eastburn, Prisoner of the Indians

Robert Eastburn was a young trader from Philadelphia who was taken prisoner while on a wagon road just north of where Rome, New York is now. In early Spring of 1756, he was traveling with a small group of men when attacked by Indians. In his journal he describes his capture and treatment on the march to the Indian village where he remained for twenty months. He was returned to Philadelphia on November 26, 1757.

Source: Spears, John R. Editor, *The Dangers, Sufferings of Robert Eastburn and His Deliverance from Indian Captivity*, Cleveland, The Burrows Brothers Co., 1904, pp. 30-43.

"...when we had advanced about a Quarter of a Mile, we heard a Shot, followed with doleful Cries of a dying Man, which excited me to advance, in order to discover the enemy, who I soon perceived were prepared to receive us: In this difficult Situation, seeing a large Pine-Tree near, I repaired to it for shelter; and while the Enemy were viewing our Party, I having a good Chance of killing two at a Shot, quickly discharged at them, but could not certainly know what Execution was done, till some time after; our Company likewise discharged, and retreated: Seeing myself in Danger of being surrounded, I was obliged to Retreat a different Course, and to my great Surprize, fell into a deep Mire, which the Enemy, by following my Track in a light Snow, soon discovered, and obliged me to surrender, to prevent a cruel Death....

Presently after I was taken, I was surrounded by a great Number, who stripped me of my Cloathing, Hat, and Neckcloth (so that I had nothing left but a Flannel Vest, without Sleeves) put a Rope on my Neck, bound my Arms fast behind me, put a long Band round my Body, and a large Pack on my Back, struck me on the Head (a severe Blow,) and drove me through the Woods before them....

When we encamped in the Evening, the commanding-Officer ordered the Indians to bring me to his Tent, and asked me, by an Interpreter, if I thought General Johnson would follow them, I told him I judged not, but rather thought he would proceed to Oswego....I informed the General, that his Indian Warriors had stripped me of my Cloathing, and would be glad if he would be good enough to order me some Relief; to which he replied, that I would get Cloaths when I came to Canada, which was cold Comfort to one almost frozen! On my Return, the Indians perceiving I was unwell, and could not eat their coarse Feed, ordered some Chocolate (which they had brought from the Carrying-Place) to be boiled for me, and seeing me eat that, appeared pleased.

A strong Guard was kept every Night; One of our Men being weakened by his Wounds, and rendered unable to keep Pace with them, was killed and scalped on the Road! - I was all this Time almost naked, traveling through deep Snow, and wading through Rivers cold as Ice!

After Seven Days March, we arrived at Lake Ontario, where I eat some Horse-Flesh, which tasted very agreeably, for the hungry Man, as Solomon observes, every bitter Thing is sweet.

The French carried several of their wounded Men all the Way upon their Backs, and (many of them wore no Breeches in their Travels in this cold Season, they are strong, hardy Men). The Indians had Three of their Party wounded, which they likewise carried on their Backs, I wish there was more of this Hardness, so necessary for War, in our Nation....

The Prisoners were so divided, that but few could Converse together on our March, and (which was still more disagreeable and distressing) an Indian, who had a large Bunch of green Scalps, taken off our Men's Heads, marched before me, and another with a sharp Spear behind, to drive me after him; by which Means, the Scalps were very often close to my Face, and as we marched, they frequently every Day gave the Dead Shout which was repeated as many Times as there were Captives and Scalps taken!

Sunday, April 11th, Set off towards Conasadauga, traveled about two Hours, and then saw the Town, over a great River, which was still frozen; the Indians stopped, and we were soon joined with a Number of our own Company, which we had not seen for several Days: The Prisoners, in Number Eight, were ordered to lay down our Packs, and be painted; the wounded Indian painted me, and put a Belt of Wampum round my Neck, instead of the Rope which I had worn 400 Miles. Then set off toward the town on the Ice, which was four Miles over; our Heads were not allowed to be covered, lest our fine Paint should be hid, the Weather in the mean time very cold, like to Freeze our Ears; after we had advanced nearer to the Town, the Indian women came out to meet us, and relieved their Husbands of their Packs.

As soon as we landed at Conasadauga, a large Body of Indians came and incompassed us round, and ordered the Prisoners to dance and sing the prisoners Song, (which I was still enabled to decline) at the conclusion of which, the Indians gave a Shout, and opened the ring to let us run, and then fell on us with their Fists, and knocked several down; in the mean Time, one ran before to direct us to an Indian House, which was open, and as soon as we got in, we were beat no more; my Head was sore with beating, and pained me several Days. The Squaws were kind to us, gave us boiled Corn and Beans to eat, and Fire to warm us...."

A Prisoner of the French

The following letter was written by a man whose name has been lost. He was a civilian aboard a British Man-of-War, The Fame, *when it was captured on May 17, 1760 by the French. He and the other prisoners were taken off* The Fame *and put on small boats to be taken to Quebec. Here is his account of their abandonment and rescue.*

Source: Knox, Captain John, *Historical Journal of the Campaigns in North America For the Years 1757, 1758, 1759, and 1760*, Toronto, The Champlain Society, 1916, pp. 403-405.

"The English prisoners were sixty men, and seven women, taken in these small vessels for Quebec. Before the English ships appeared we were well used; but on their coming in sight, we were put into the hold of a small *schooner*, without air, without light, strongly guarded by a party of soldiers, under the cannon of the battery; our cloaths and beds taken from us; we had not room to stretch ourselves along on a tier of casks, which remained in the hold. This misery we suffered five days, and had very little provisions, and only brackish water to drink; then we were transported into the hold of the *frigate*, and worse treated there: the sailors were put into irons, and the captains and merchants had an old sail to lie on, spread on a row of *hogsheads*. Our allowance was bread and wine, with two ounces of pork per day; but, thank God, our appetites were not very keen; and if we complained that we were stifled with stench and heat, and eat up with vermin, they silenced us with saying, "Well, you shall go on shore under a guard of Indians," after telling us the savages had sworn they would scalp us every soul: they told us also, that, if we made the least noise, they would point four cannon into the hold and sink the vessel, or burn us like a parcel of rats.

When we begged for one of our own shirts, for God's sake, they said they were too busy to mind us. We remained seven days in this condition; and when they saw our vessels hard after them, they confined us in the hold of the Marquis de Malos; and on the second or third day of our confinement, we heard the engagement, and, by two terrible reports, we understood the vessels of the French were blown up. Immediately after, we were ordered upon deck, and desired to embark upon a raft, which would have sunk with one half of our number; but we resisted, and would not go, for fear of the Indians: they told us then the vessel was ours, and desired us to take our chance; and then a guard of soldiers forced us into the hold, and overlaid the hatches, and left us.

Some time after, growing uneasy, and almost mad with fear, expecting every moment to be blown up, we knocked down a large bulkhead, and forced up the hatches, and set ourselves at liberty; and on rummaging the hold, to look for fire laid for us, we found an old English pendant, which we hoisted, that the English might observe us; but the smoke of the other two ships burning between us, hindered them from seeing us: all the shore was lined with Indians, firing small arms upon us; but, thank God, we were out of the reach of muskets. We were in the utmost perplexity to get away, because we knew, had we remained aboard that night, we should have been boarded by the Indians, and every man scalped.

We searched the ship for arms, but found none. We got a *hogshead* of scalping-knives, and every man took one, and armed with sticks and cannon-shot, we determined to stand on our defence to the last, if we could not escape. We hoisted a sail upon the raft, and enlarged it, determined to pass the battery, and get to the English ships before night; but, happy for us, a young fellow who could swim very well, set off, and arrived safe at The Repulse, which was a full league distant from our prison; and immediately nine boats were manned, and bravely passed the battery in spite of a brisk cannonading from it; the Repulse and Scarborough covered the boats, and plied the fort so successfully, that they abandoned it, and left us masters. Capt. Wood of the marines was my deliverer on the 8th of July; he commanded one of the boats, and took me on board, and brought me safe into his ship."

The Ticonderoga Campaigns

Peter Pond's Account of the 1758 Campaign

Although Peter Pond is better known for his accounts of his experiences as a fur trader and explorer after the French and Indian War, his journal opens with his reminiscences of Connecticut farm life. His longing for more colorful experiences led him to volunteer for several expeditions.

We do not know exactly how Americans spoke in the 18th century, but Pond's spelling gives the reader many clues, especially if read aloud. These passages should be read at least twice; the first time to decode the sometimes quaint but invariably phonetic spelling; the second and subsequent times for comprehension. His journal reveals a man of intelligence, wit, and humor. It is fast-paced and makes for capital reading. One can imagine the discussion (or arguments) as Pond and his father wrestled with the boy's determination to "....be a Solge."

On the seventh and eighth of July, 1758, Pond took part in the British attempt to take Fort Carillon, as Ticonderoga was called by the French. General Abercromby insisted on attacking the fort in traditional European manner. The result, as Peter Pond relates, was disastrous. The brilliant popular Lord Howe was killed. Abercromby was replaced by the more able Lord Jeffrey Amherst. The next year the British did take the fort, as the Reverend Henry True relates in a letter to his wife. Reverend True was a minister from New Hampshire serving with a New Hampshire unit.

Here follows the young volunteer Peter Pond's account of the first attempt to take the French stronghold.

Source: *Five Fur Traders of the Northwest*, edited by C. M. Gates, U of Minn. Press, 1933, pp. 19-23.

"The year insewing which was 57 I taread at home with my Parans so that I ascaped the Misfortune of a number of my Countrey men for Moncalm came against fort George & Capterd it & as the amaracans ware Going of for fort Edwaud a Greabel [agreeable] to ye Capatalasion [capitulation] the Indians fel apon them and mad grate Havack.

In ye year 58 the Safety of British Amaraca required that a large Arme should be raised to act with the British Troops against Cannaday and under the command of Gineral Abercrombie against ticonderoge. I found tareing at home was too Inactive a Life for me therefore I joined many of my old Companyans a secont time for the Arme of ye end of the Campain under the same officers and same Regiment under the command of Cornl Nathan Whiting. In the Spring we embarked to gine the Arme at Albany whare we arrived safe at the time appointed. We ware emploid in forwarding Provishuns to Fort Edward for the youse of the Sarvis. When all was readey to cross Lake George the Armey Imbarked consisting of 18000 British & Provincals in about 1200 Boates and a number of whalebotes, floating Battery, Gondaloes, Rogelleyes & Gunbotes. The next day we arrived at the North end of Lake George and landed without opposition. The french that were encampt at that end of the Lake fled at our appearance as far as Ticonderoge and joined thare old commander Moncalm & we ware drawn up in order and divided in Collams and ordered to March toward Montcalm in his camp before the fort — but unfortunately for us Moncalm like a Gineral dispatched Five hundred to oppose us in our landing or at least to Imbarres us in our March so he might put his Camp in some sort of defense before our Arme could arrive & thay did it most completely. We had not Marcht more than a Mile & a Half Befoare we Meat the falon Hope for Such it Proved to be. The British troops Kept [the] Rode in One Collam the Amara Cans Marcht threw ye Woods on thare Left. On ye Rite of the British was the Run of Water that Emteys from Lake George into Lake Champlain. The British &

French Meat in the Open Rode Verey near Each Other Befoar thay Discovered the french On a Count of the Uneaveneas of the Ground. Lord How held the secont Place in Command & Beaing at the Head of the British troops with a small sidearm in his hand he Ordered the troopes to forme thare front to ye Left to atack the french But While this Was Dueing the french fird & his Lordship Receaved a Ball & three Buck shot threw the Senter of his Brest & Expired without Spekeing a word. But the french Pade Dear for this bold atempt. It Was But a Short time Befoare thay ware Surounded By the Hole of the Amaracan troops & those that Did not Lepe into the Raped [rapid] Stream in Order to Regan thare Camp ware Made Prisners or Kild & those that Did Went Down with the Raped Curant & Was Drounded. From the Best Information I Could Geat from ye french of that Partea was that thare was But Seven men of ye five Hundred that Reacht the Campt But it answerd the Purpas Amaseingly. This afair Hapend on thirsday. The troops Beaing all Strangers to the Ground & Runing threw the Woods after the Disparst frenchmen Night came on and they Got thmSelves so Disparst that thay could not find the way Back to thare Boates at the Landing. That Nite the British did Beatter haveing the Open Rod to Direct them thay Got to ye Lake Sid Without trubel. A Large Party of ye amaracans Past the Nite within a Bout half a Mile of the french Lines With Out noeing whare they ware til Morning. I was not in this Partey. I had wanderd in ye Woods in the Nite with A Bout twelve Men of my aquantans — finealey fel on the Rode a Bout a Mile North of ye spot whare the first fire began. Being in the Rode we Marched toward Our boates at ye Water Side But Being Dark we Made But a Stumbling Pece of Bisness of it & Sun Coming aMong the Dead Bodeyes Which ware Strewed Quit thick on the Ground for Sum Little Distans. We Stumbled over them for a while as long as thay Lasted. At Lengh we Got to the Water just Before Day Lite in the Morn. What could be found of the troops Got in sum Order & Began our March a Bout two a Clock in ye Afternoon Crossing the Raped Stream & Left it on Our Left the rode on this Side was Good & we advansd toward the french Camp as fars the Miles [Mills] About a Mile from the Works & thare Past the Night

Lying on Our Armes. This Delay Gave the french What thay Wanted — time to secure thare Camp which was well Executed. The Next Day which was Satterday about Eleven we ware Seat in Mosin the British Leading the Van it was about. Thay ware Drawn up Before Strong Brest Work but more in Extent then to Permit four thousand five Hundred acting. We had no Cannon up the works. The Intent was to March over this work But thay found themselves Sadly Mistaken. The french had Cut Down a Grate number of Pinetrease in front of thare Camp at som distance. While som ware Entrenching Others ware Imploiyed Cuting of the Lims of the Trease and Sharpening them at Both Ends for a *Shevoe Dufrease,*[1] other Cuting of Larg Logs and Geting them to the Brest Works. At Lengh thay ware Ready for Our Resaption. About twelve the Parties Began thare fire & the British Put thare Plan on fut to March Over the Works But the Lims and tops of the Trease on the Side for the Diek Stuck fast in the Ground and all pointed at upper End that thay Could not Git threw them til thay ware at Last Obliged to Quit that plan for three forths ware Kild in the atempt But the Grater Part of the armey Lad in the Rear on thare fases til Nite while the British ware Batteling a Brest work Nine Logs thick in Som plases which was Dun without ye Help of Canan tho we had as fine an Artilrey Just at Hand as Could be in an armey of fifteen thousand Men But thay ware of no youse while thay ware Lying on thare fases. Just as the sun was Seating Abercrombie came from left to Rite in the rear of the troops ingaged and Ordered a Retreat Beat and we left the Ground with about two thousand two hundred Loss as I was Informed By an Officer who saw the Returns of ye Nite Wounded and Mising. We ware Ordered to Regain our Boates at the Lake Side which was Dun after traveling all Nite so Sloley that we fell asleep by the Way. About Nine or tenn in the Morning we ware Ordered to Imbark & Cross the Lake to the Head of Lake George But to Sea the Confuson thare was the Solgers Could not find thare One Botes But Imbarked Permisherley [promiscuously]

[1] A corruption of the French term: chevaux de frise: a formidible barrier made of sticks sharpened at both ends and driven through a horizontal shaft at right angles. It would be almost impossible to climb over.

whare Ever thay Could Git in expecting the french at thare Heales Eaverey minnet. We arivd at the Head of the Lake in a short time — took up our Old Incampment which was well fortefied. After a few Days the armey Began to Com to themselves and found thay ware safe for the hold of the french in that Part of the Country was not more than three thousand men and we about fortee thousand. We then Began to Git up Provishan from fort Edward to the Camp But the french ware so Bold as to Beseat our Scouting Partey Between the Camp and fort Edward & Cut of all the teames, Destroy the provishun, Kill the Parties and all under thare ascort. We Past the Sumer in that Maner & in the fall Verey late the Camp Broke up and what Remaned Went into Winter Qaters in Differant Parts of the Collanees. Thus Ended the Most Ridicklas Campane Eaver Hard of."

Henry True's Account of the 1759 Campaign

Here is the letter Reverend Henry True sent to his wife Ruth from Albany on 30 July, 1759.

Source: *Journals and Letters of Rev. Henry True*, Special Collections CIHM 44745, Stauffer Library, Queen's University, Kingston, Ontario, Canada.

My Dear Spouse:

Amidst other writing I cannot cease to write to you, hoping these will find you well and our children, &c. I have through the goodness of God injoyed a good state of health since I left you....

Saturday, July 21st - Two o'clock in ye morning the encampment struck ye tents, by break of day we got on board *Batteaus* about twelve thousand, with a propitious gale we passed Lake George within about 2 miles where they landed last year, out of ye view of that place, there we lay all night upon our oars, wind something high weather lowering. In ye morning, July 22d. it cleared off pleasant; ye army, after getting into regular order, heaven governing ye wind and ye weather, we landed about 10 o'clock, about ye time when ye assembly of God's people were praying for us. We expected to meet ye enemy at landing, but they did not oppose our landing; after landing immediately some of our men marched to ye sawmill, there they surrounded about 20 French and Indians. We killed some of them and took 2 prisoners, ye rest fleeing, for they came out only to make discoveries as they say, it being rumored yt we were actually coming; our men immediately took possession of ye breast works where ye men were slaughtered last year, confining ye enemy all in ye fort; they attempted to make a sally or two but were soon repulsed, our men proceed immediately to entrench, the enemy continually kept firing ball and bombs, but they did but very little harm to us. The General was present and was ready to say that ye French bombs could not hurt us....

July 28th, at night when we had got our artilery ready to play, the enemy blew up ye magazine and so fled all of them to about 30 which we took, they left some cannons, some mortars and balls, and what number I can't certainly learn. New Hampshire regiment being ordered by ye General to march back to Albany, to Schenectady, to Oswego; the General thinking they might be needing to aid Br. General Prideaux that has gone against Niagara, that we were to help finish a fort yt is erecting at Oswego....

If I really thought it duty and subservient to ye common cause not to proceed, I should seek for a discharge, but I am apprehensive my presence is needful at this juncture...in haste, desiring a constant remembrance in your prayers to God yt I may ever be resigned to his will and may be enabled to glorifie him whether it be by life or by death, remain your loving husband till death.

Henry True

Ye regiment in general healthy, all from Hampstead are well, but one died, one Haswell, an aged man from Kingston."

The Legend of Ticonderoga

Fort Ticonderoga on Lake Champlain guards the narrows of the lake. (Detail from a photo by William A. Pollman)

The popular Scottish poet Robert Louis Stevenson became fascinated by a legend that grew up about Major Duncan Campbell of the famous Black Watch, 42nd Highland Regiment. Over two-thirds of these brave soldiers lost their lives at Ticonderoga in the battle so vividly described by Peter Pond in his Journal which appears on pages 36 to 39. Among the casualties was Major Campbell. Here is his story and the poem which it inspired. Although Robert Louis Stevenson changed the names, the poem is really about Major Duncan Campbell of Inverawe, Scotland.

Long before Campbell was sent to America as a member of the Black Watch Regiment, a stranger appeared at his door and begged for sanctuary. He said that he had just killed a man in a fair fight. Campbell agreed to shelter him, but soon afterwards discovered that the man who had been killed was Campbell's own cousin. In Scotland, once a person offers sanctuary, he is bound to provide it, even though in this case, he was torn between that promise and loyalty to his family which, by custom, demanded that he avenge his cousin's death. During a night of restless sleep, he awoke to find his cousin's ghost standing by his bed, saying, "Inverawe! Inverawe! Blood has been shed. Shield not the murdered!"

The next day Campbell tried to get the stranger to leave, but he refused and reminded his host of his promise. However, Campbell convinced the murderer that he should go to a cave to hide. Campbell led him to the cave and left him there. That night the apparition appeared again with the same message. When Campbell went to the cave in the morning the man was gone. The ghost appeared a third time that night, but with a different message. In a hollow voice, he said, "Farewell, Inverawe! Farewell, 'till we meet at Ticonderoga!' "

"Ticonderoga" meant nothing to a Scottish highlander and so, with time, the awful message dimmed in the mind of Duncan Campbell. He came to America with his regiment. The French had built a fort between Lake Champlain and Lake George which they named Fort Carrillon. It is not known whether the Major knew that the traditional name of that strategic spot was Ticonderoga. But on the day of the attack on Fort Carillon, he told his fellow officers that his cousin's ghost had come to his tent in the night, telling him that he was at last at Ticonderoga and that he would die. His arm was shattered during the battle. He was taken back to Fort Edward but died nine days later. He is buried in a cemetery just north of the village of Fort Edward, not far from Ticonderoga.

Ticonderoga

by

Robert Louis Stevenson

Source: *The Works of Robert Louis Stevenson*, Vol. 8, National Library Co, NY, 1906, pp. 197-207.

This is the tale of the man
  Who heard a word in the night
In the land of the heathery hills
  In the days of the feud and the fight.
By the sides of the rainy sea,
  Where never a stranger came,
On the awful lips of the dead,
  He heard the outlandish name.
It sang in his sleeping ears,
  It hummed in his waking head:
The name — Ticonderoga,
  The utterance of the dead.

I. THE SAYING OF THE NAME

On the loch-sides of Appin,
  When the mist blew from the sea,
A Stewart stood with a Cameron:
  An angry man was he.
The blood beat in his ears,
  The blood ran hot to his head,
The mist blew from the sea,
  And there was the Cameron dead.
"O, what have I done to my friend,
  O, what have I done to mysel',
That he should be cold and dead,
  And I in the danger of all?

Nothing but danger about me,
  Nothing behind and before,
Death at wait in the heather
  In Appin and Mamore,
Hate at all of the ferries
  And death at each of the fords,
Camerons priming gunlocks
  And Camerons sharpening swords."

But this was a man of counsel,
  This was a man of a score,
There dwelt no pawkier Stewart
  In Appin or Mamore.
He looked on the blowing mist,
  He looked on the awful dead,
And there came a smile on his face
  And there slipped a thought in his head.

Out over cairn and moss,
  Out over scrog and scaur,
He ran as runs the clansman
  That bears the cross of war.
His heart beat in his body,
  His hair clove to his face,
When he came at last in the gloaming
  To the dead man's brother's place.
The east was white with the moon,
  The west with the sun was red,
And there, in the house-doorway,
  Stood the brother of the dead.

"I have slain a man to my danger,
  I have slain a man to my death.
I put my soul in your hands,"
  The panting Stewart saith.
"I lay it bare in your hands,
  For I know your hands are leal;
And be you my targe and bulwark
  From the bullet and the steel."

Then up and spoke the Cameron,
  And gave him his hand again:
"There shall never a man in Scotland
  Set faith in me in vain;
And whatever man you have slaughtered,
  Of whatever name or line,
By my sword and yonder mountain,
  I make your quarrel mine.
I bid you to my fireside,
  I share with you house and hall;
It stands upon my honour
  To see you safe from all."

It fell in the time of midnight,
  When the fox barked in the den
And the plaids were over the faces
  In all the houses of men,
That as the living Cameron
  Lay sleepless on his bed,
Out of the night and the other world,
  Came in to him the dead.

"My blood is on the heather,
  My bones are on the hill;
There is joy in the home of ravens
  That the young shall eat their fill.
My blood is poured in the dust,
  My soul is spilled in the air;
And the man that has undone me
  Sleeps in my brother's care."

"I'm wae for your death, my brother,
  But if all of my house were dead,
I couldnae withdraw the plighted hand,
  Nor break the word once said."

"O, what shall I say to our father,
  In the place to which I fare?
O, what shall I say to our mother,
  Who greets to see me there?
And to all the kindly Camerons
  That have lived and died long-syne —
Is this the word you send them,
  Fause-hearted brother mine?"

"It's neither fear nor duty,
  It's neither quick nor dead
Shall gar me withdraw the plighted hand,
  Or break the word once said."

Thrice in the time of midnight,
  When the fox barked in the den,
And the plaids were over the faces
  In all the houses of men,
Thrice as the living Cameron
  Lay sleepless on his bed,
Out of the night and the other world
  Came in to him the dead,
And cried to him for vengeance
  On the man that laid him low;
And thrice the living Cameron
  Told the dead Cameron, no.

"Thrice have you seen me, brother,
  But now shall see me no more,
Till you meet your angry fathers
  Upon the farther shore.
Thrice have I spoken, and now,
  Before the cock be heard,
I take my leave for ever
  With the naming of a word.
It shall sing in your sleeping ears,
  It shall hum in your waking head,
The name — Ticonderoga,
  And the warning of the dead."

Now when the night was over
  And the time of people's fears,
The Cameron walked abroad,
  And the word was in his ears.
"Many a name I know,
  But never a name like this;
O, where shall I find a skilly man
  Shall tell me what it is?"
With many a man he counselled
  Of high and low degree,
With the herdsmen on the mountains
  And the fishers of the sea.
And he came and went unweary,
  And read the books of yore,
And the runes that were written of old
  On the stones upon the moor.
And many a name he was told,
  But never the name of his fears —
Never, in east or west,
  The name that rang in his ears:
Names of men and of clans;
  Names for the grass and the tree,
For the smallest tarn in the mountains,
  The smallest reef in the sea:
Names for the high and low,
  The names of the craig and the flat;
But in all the land of Scotland,
  Never a name like that.

II. THE SEEKING OF THE NAME

And now there was speech in the south,
  And a man of the south that was wise,
A periwig'd lord of London,
  Called on the clans to rise.
And the riders rode, and the summons
  Came to the western shore,
To the land of the sea and the heather,
  To Appin and Mamore.
It called on all to gather
  From every scrog and scaur,
That loved their fathers' tartan
  And the ancient game of war.
And down the watery valley
  And up the windy hill,
Once more, as in the olden,
  The pipes were sounding shrill;
Again in highland sunshine
  The naked steel was bright;
And the lads, once more in tartan,
  Went forth again to fight.

"O, why should I dwell here
  With a weird upon my life,
When the clansmen shout for battle
  And the war-swords clash in strife?
I cannae joy at feast,
  I cannae sleep in bed,
For the wonder of the word
  And the warning of the dead.
It sings in my sleeping ears
  It hums in my waking head,
The name — Ticonderoga,
  The utterance of the dead.

Then up, and with the fighting men
  To march away from here,
Till the cry of the great war-pipe
  Shall drown it in my ear!"

Where flew King George's ensign
  The plaided soldiers went:
They drew the sword in Germany,
  In Flanders pitched the tent.
The bells of foreign cities
  Rang far across the plain:
They passed the happy Rhine,
  They drank the rapid Main.
Through Asiatic jungles
  The Tartans filed their way,
And the neighing of the warpipes
  Struck terror in Cathay.

"Many a name have I heard," he thought,
  "In all the tongues of men,
Full many a name both here and there,
  Full many both now and then.
When I was at home in my father's house
  In the land of the naked knee,
Between the eagles that fly in the lift
  And the herrings that swim in the sea,
And now that I am a captain-man
  With a braw cockade in my hat —
Many a name have I heard," he thought,
  "But never a name like that."

III. THE PLACE OF THE NAME

There fell a war in a woody place,
  Lay far across the sea,
A war of the march in the mirk midnight
  And the shot from behind the tree,
The shaven head and the painted face,
  The silent foot in the wood,
In a land of a strange, outlandish tongue
  That was hard to be understood.

It fell about the gloaming
  The general stood with his staff,
He stood and he looked east and west
  With little mind to laugh.
"Far have I been and much have I seen,
  And kent both gain and loss,
But here we have woods on every hand
  And a kittle water to cross.
Far have I been and much have I seen,
  But never the beat of this;
And there's one must go down to that waterside
  To see how deep it is."

It fell in the dusk of the night
  When unco things betide,
The skilly captain, the Cameron,
  Went down to that waterside.
Canny and soft the captain went;
  And a man of the woody land,
With the shaven head and the painted face,
  Went down at his right hand.
It fell in the quiet night,
  There was never a sound to ken;
But all of the woods to the right and left
  Lay filled with the painted men.

"Far have I been and much have I seen
  Both as a man and boy,
But never have I set forth a foot
  On so perilous an employ."
It fell in the dusk of the night
  When unco things betide,
That he was aware of a captain-man
  Drew near to the waterside.
He was aware of his coming
  Down in the gloaming alone;
And he looked in the face of the man
  And lo! the face was his own.
"This is my weird," he said,
  "And now I ken the worst;
For many shall fall the morn,
  But I shall fall with the first.
O, you of the outland tongue,
  You of the painted face,
This is the place of my death;
  Can you tell me the name of the place?'
"Since the Frenchmen have been here
  They have called it Sault-Marie;
But that is a name for priests
  And for not you and me.
It went by another word,"
  Quoth he of the shaven head:
"It was called Ticonderoga
  In the days of the great dead."

And it fell on the morrow's morning,
  In the fiercest of the fight,
That the Cameron bit the dust
  As he foretold at night;
And far from the hills of heather,
  Far from the isles of the sea,
He sleeps in the place of the name
  As it was doomed to be.

The Siege of Quebec

Throughout the summer, the British tried to take Quebec, but in spite of continuous shelling, they were unable to take the city. Quebec City had natural defenses on two sides: high cliffs, and the Montmorency River. On the other side, the city had dense stone walls, and mounted cannons. To take Quebec, General James Wolfe commanded an army of over 9,000 regulars, 22 warships, and 119 transports.

The following are notes regarding the defense of Quebec made by M. de Montcalm in the early summer of 1759. It is obvious that he realizes the importance of keeping this city. The general tone of the notes conveys a feeling of urgency, lack of optimism and even, at times, near desperation.

Marquis de Montcalm

Major General James Wolfe

Montcalm's Defense

Source: Knox, John, *Historical Journal of the Canpaigns in North America for the Years 1757, 1758, 1759, and 1760*, Vol III, "Notes on the Defense of Quebec by the M. de Montcalm, pp. 179-182, translated from the French by Margaret Terrell.

"31 May 1759

The welfare of the colony depends mainly on the success of one battle. All our efforts should be directed as to not dividing our forces and not doing unnecessary labor, which will achieve little and fatigue our soldiers, who should be protected, so as not to enfeeble the army."

Montcalm proceeds to give orders. "...here are the most pressing things that need to be done, and to which we need to use all hands possible, without losing a moment, and to assign the various jobs not only to the engineers and officers of the artillery; but to certain officers capable of executing the following:

1. Work on bridges on the three rivers: St. Charles, Cap Rouge, and J. Cartier.
2. Work to secure the head of the bridge.
3. Establish two battlements and set up gun batteries.
4. Use all hands possible to close off as best possible the high and low of the town.

   We consider that the lower town will never be fully secure — but it must at least look to the enemy that to attack it will be difficult and deadly.
5. Place all batteries in such a way as to be able to help those already in place in the lower town.
6. Give as many of the Canadians as possible tools...for the construction of floating batteries, boats carrying cannon-boats with fire works.

   ....all who are capable must work - all in the colony and the Canadians, and to use them as of tomorrow alongside the officers, and to not start any job which they will not finish.

Once these jobs are done, we can use all the troops and Canadians to build a redout at the head of the St. Charles River — and entrenchments at all areas of said river where at all possible.

All other works seem to me useless, as we have neither the time or the means to do all projected....We must await the enemy with much calm and courage....

June 28 1759

The front line of the enemy is now 15 leagues from us. We do not know what they have behind which can join them from one moment to another. Our army will not be regrouped and in a fighting state for 15 days. If the enemy comes sooner, what will be our salvation? It will not be the defense of the town, it will be the success of the brulots [burning shafts launched from boats]....

Send parties by land with the Canadians and Indians. If there are no Canadian officers to lead them, I offer MM de La Rochebeaucourt, Calan, and other officers of the land troops, who would ask nothing better than to have Canadians as guides....Dumas should, as of today, arrange by companies, all who are able to fight inside the town, and to assign to them officers of the militia, or prominent civilians, until we have available regular officers. I believe that it would be an advantage to form companies of Canadian volunteers.

This is my order this AM the 28th.

Montcalm"

Montcalm repulsed all attempts of the British until September. By early September, General Wolfe knew that soon he would have to take his ships away or they would be frozen into the ice of the river. He decided to make one last attempt to take the city. He took a group of small boats into a narrow cove, out of sight of the French. A sentry heard a noise and challenged them, but a quick-thinking French-speaking British officer answered. His response was accepted, the boats landed, and the Regulars scaled the cliffs.

Early morning of September 13, 1759 found the British lined up on the Plains of Abraham, an area west of the city. A French force, under the command of the Marquis de Montcalm, hurriedly marched out to meet the enemy.

General Wolfe Adresses His Troops

The thirty-two-year-old General Wolfe made a stirring address to his troops as they waited for the French to attack. His speech ended with a prophetic statement:

Source: Knox's Historical Journal, *op. cit.*, General Wolfe To His Army, p. 335.

"I congratulate you, my brave countrymen, & fellow Soldiers! on the spirit and Success with which you have executed this important part of our enterprise. The formidable Heights of Abraham are now surmounted; and the City of Quebec, the object of all our toils, now stands in full view before us. A perfidious enemy, who have dared to exasperate you by their cruelties, but not to oppose you on equal ground, are now constrained to face you on the open plain, without ramparts or entrenchments to shelter them....

This day puts it into your power to terminate the fatigues of a Siege which has so long employed your courage and patience. Possessed with a full confidence of the certain success which British valour must gain over such enemies, I have led you up to these steep and dengerous rocks; only solicitous to shew you the foe within your reach. The impossibility of a retreat makes no difference in the situation of men resolved to conquer or die: and, believe me, my friends if your conquest could be bought with the blood of your general, he would most cheerfully resign a life which he has long devoted to his country."

General Wolfe walked up and down along the front lines, armed only with a cane raised high in the air. Finally, by lowering it, he gave the order to return fire when the French troops were only forty yards away. Wolfe was shot several times. When told that the French were running he smiled and said, "God be praised. I will die in peace."

Montcalm was also mortally wounded. When his doctor told him that he had only a few hours to live, he said, "So much the better. I will not see the surrender of Quebec."

The short battle that took place on the morning of 13th September 1759 was a turning point of the war, as M. de Montcalm well knew it would be.

The Ruins of Notre Dame des Victoires, Quebec, 1759

A Nun's Account of the Siege of Quebec

This is an account of the siege of Quebec by an unidentified nun writing to her Mother Superior. This Sister was apparently in charge of General Hospital, which was about a half mile from the city walls. Her account of the Siege gives us a graphic picture from an entirely different perspective. She is not a scout, a soldier, or an officer. Her report, rather, describes how these devoted women dealt with enormous problems. They cared for the sick and wounded French, and later British. The overcrowding reached gigantic proportions, not just in the hospital, but in the convent — as nuns from three other convents joined them. They also had to accommodate citizens who had stayed in Quebec rather than flee to Montreal or Three Rivers. The nuns had to deal with hunger and even starvation, the shelling of the city, and their own terror, as the British approached and then entered the hospital.

Throughout the letter, the Sister struggles to be fair and to find goodness wherever she can, even stating that the British were "...the most moderate of conquerors." But she cannot resist saying, "However, their good treatment of us has not yet dried our tears." And although the British offered their protection, and some provisions, they brought their sick and wounded, thus imposing even greater hardship on the nuns. To make matters worse, French soldiers took livestock and grain from property of the nuns outside the city. And still the numbers of sick and wounded at the hospital grew. At one point, the French commander, M. de Levi, contemplated destroying the hospital itself. Finally, she tells the Mother Superior that the French have refused to pay them for caring for the French troops. Most readers will be moved by the account of this gentle woman faced with the realities and the horrors of war.

Source: *Nun of the General Hospital of Quebec: Siege of Quebec of 1759*, Special Collections CIHM 52446, Stauffer Library, Queen's University, Kingston, Ontario, Canada, pp. 6-21.

"The only rest we partook of was during prayers, and still it was not without interruption from the noise of shells and shot, dreading every moment that they would be directed towards us. The red-hot shot and carcasses terrified those who attended the sick during the night. They had the affliction of witnessing the destruction of the houses of the citizens....During one night, upwards of fifty of the best homes in the Lower Town were destroyed....

In addition to these misfortunes, we had to contend with more than one enemy; famine, at all times inseparable from war, threatened to reduce us to the last extremity; upwards of six hundred persons in our building and vicinity, partaking of our small means of subsistence, supplied from the government stores, which were likely soon to be short of what was required for the troops....

Our enemy, informed of our destitute condition, was satisfied with battering our walls, despairing of vanquishing us, except by starvation....

After remaining in vain nearly three months at anchor in the Port, they [British] appeared disposed to retire, despairing of success; but the Almighty, whose intentions are beyond our penetration, and always just, having resolved to subdue us, inspired the English Commander with the idea of making another attempt before his departure, which was done by surprise during the night. It was the intention, that night, to send supplies to a body of troops forming an outpost on the heights near Quebec. A miserable deserter gave the information to the enemy, and persuaded them that is would be easy to surprise us, and pass their boats by using our countersign. They profited by the information and the treasonable scheme succeeded. They landed on giving the password; the officer detected the deceit, but too late. He defended his post bravely with his small band, and was wounded. By this plan the enemy found themselves on the heights near the city. General De Montcalm, without loss of time, marched at the head of his army; but having to proceed about half a league, the enemy had time to bring up their artillery, and to form for the reception of the French. Our leading batallions did not wait the arrival and formation of the other forces to support them, they rushed with their usual impetuosity on their enemies and killed a great number; but they were soon overcome by the artillery. They lost their General and a great number of officers. Our loss was not equal to that of the enemy; but it was not the less serious. General De Montcalm and his principal officers fell on the occasion.

Several officers of the Canadian Militia, fathers of families, shared the same fate. We witnessed the carnage from our windows. It was in such a scene that charity triumphed, and caused us to forget self-preservation and the danger we were exposed to, in the immediate presence of the enemy. We were in the midst of the dead and dying, who were brought in to us by hundreds, many of them our close connexions; it was necessary to smother our griefs and exert ourselves to relieve them. Loaded with the inmates of three convents, and all the inhabitants of the neighbouring suburbs, which the approach of the enemy caused to fly in this direction, you may judge of our terror and confusion. The enemy masters of the field, and within a few paces of our house. Exposed to the fury of the soldiers, we had reason to dread the worst. It was then that we experienced the truth of the words of holy writ: "he who places his trust in the Lord has nothing to fear.".....

But tho' not wanting in faith or hope, the approach of night greatly added to our fears. The three sisterhoods, with the exception of those who were dispersed over the house, prostrated themselves at the foot of the altar, to implore Divine mercy. The silence and consternation which prevailed, was suddenly interrupted by loud and repeated knocks at our doors. Two young Nuns, who were carrying broth to the sick, unavoidably happened to be near when the door was opened. The palor and fright which overcame them, touched the officer, and he prevented the guard from entering; he demanded the appearance of the superiors, and desired them to assure us of protection; he said that part of the English force would entour and take possession of the house, apprehending that our army, which was not distant, might return and attack them, in their intrenchments; — which would certainly have taken place had our troops been enabled to reassemble before the capitulation. Soon after we saw their army drawn up under our windows. The loss we had sustained the day before led us to fear, with reason, that our fate was decided, our people being unable to rally....

The English readily accorded the articles demanded, religious toleration and civil advantages for the inhaabitants. Happy in having acquired possession of a country, in which they had on several previous occasions failed, they were the most moderate of conquerors. We could not, without injustice, complain of the manner in which they treated us. However, their good treatment has not yet dried our tears....

The reduction of Quebec, on the 18th September, 1759, produced no tranquillity for us, but rather increased our labours. The English Generals came to our Hospital and assured us of their protection, and at the same time, required us to take charge of their wounded and sick....

The Sisters from the other Convents determined to return to their former dwellings. It was very painful for us to part with them. Their long residence with us, and the esteem and affection created thereby caused our separation to be most sensibly felt. The Rev'd Mother St. Helen, Superior, observing us overwhelmed with work, which was daily augmenting, left us twelve of her dear-Sisters, who were a great relief to us. Two of the Ursuline Sisters were too weak to be removed, and they terminated their days with us. The fatigues and sickness they endured, with much patience and resignation, merited I trust, an eternal reward. The departure of the dear Sisters, gave us no additional space, as it became necessary to place the sick of the English army in the same apartments.

Let us now return to the French. Our Generals not finding their force sufficient to undertake the recovery of their losses, proceeded to the construction of a Fort, about five leagues above Quebec, and left a garrison therein, capable of checking the enemy from penetrating into the country. They did not remain inactive, but were constantly on the alert, harassing the enemy. The English were not safe beyond the gates of Quebec. General Murray the commander of the place, on several occasions was near being made a prisoner; and would not have escaped if our people had been faithful. Prisoners were frequently made, which so irritated the commander, that he sent out detachments to pillage and burn the habitations of the country people....

The French forces did not spare the inhabitants of the country; they lived freely at the expense of those unfortunate people. We suffered considerable loss in a Seigneurie which we possessed below Quebec. The officer commanding seized on all our cattle, which were numerous, and wheat to subsist his troops. The purveyor rendered us no account of such seizures. Notwhithstanding this loss, we were compelled to maintain up-wards of three hundred wounded, sent to us after the battle of the 13th September.

The stores of the French government, now in the possession of the English, being exhausted, we were therefore obliged to have recourse to the enemy. They gave us flour and clothing. But how little suited was it for our unfortunate wounded! We had no wine nor other comforts to afford them. Drained long since by the great numbers, nothing remained but good will. This however did not satisfy them. Our officers represented to the English commander that they were not accustomed to be treated in that manner by the King of France. The Commander, piqued by this reproach, attached the blame to us, and required us to make a statement of what was necessary for the relief of these gentlemen, and then caused us to pay for it. We flattered ourselves that the French government, more just, would be proud to reimburse all our extra expenses, which were unavoidable at this time. The desire to obtain our rights and recover the country, induced us to do our utmost in support of the cause....

We have at this time upwards of two hundred English, who occupy our dining rooms and dormitories; and as many French, in our infirmaries, leaving us merely one small room to retire into....After having prepared upwards of five hundred beds, which were procured from the public stores, as many more were required. — Our stables and barns, were filled with these unfortunate men. It was very difficult to find time to attend to all. We had in our Infirmaries seventy-two officers, thirty-three of whom died. We saw nothing but amputation of legs and arms. To crown our distress there was a deficiency of linen; we were under the necessity of giving our sheets and our body-linen....

Alas! Dear Mothers, it was a great misfortune for us that France could not send, in the spring, some vessels with provisions and munitions; we should still be under her dominion. She has lost a vast country and a faithful people, sincerely attached to their soverign; a loss we must greatly deplore, on account of our religion, and the difference of the laws to which we must submit....

You must, no doubt, have learnt, that the English, moved by our importunities, have granted us a Bishop for this unfortunate colony....

Without his protection and intercession our convent and property would have been sold to satisfy the debts, contracted to support the French troops; our creditors were compelled by order of the English Governor, to desist from their persecutions. To him our establishment is indebted for its present existence. The French government is inbebted to us in the sum of one hundred and twenty thousand livers, for expenses incurred in the maintenance of French troops. We look for no compensation for our services, He to whom we devote ourselves will recompence us amply. It is said that we will have to depend upon the public for support: we cannot believe it, as the English government, having witnessed the expenses we have incurred, will plead our cause with France, and not allow us to suffer such serious loss."

The letter ends here.

Colonel Williamson's Account of the Quebec Campaign

Source: Knox, John, *Historical Journal of the Campaigns in North America for the Years 1757, 1758, 1759, and 1760*, Vol III, "Extract from Letter of Colonel Williamson addressed to the Right Honble and Honble the Lieutenant General and Rest of the Principal Officers of His Majesty's Ordnance, Sept. 20, 1759," in the Appendix, pp. 339-340.

"I sincerely congratulate you on our success in taking Quebec at last through our perseverance and a lucky dernier effort of our very good General Wolfe, poor man being kill'd in the Field of Battle did not enjoy the fruits of his scheme well laid, which with all our hearts we prosecuted speedily which was the means of our coming so soon to a period of what a week before we did not expect....We attacked with a few of our field pieces (I should have said we prepared expecting they would attack us) the enemy in an open spott of ground called Plains of Abraham and a fair battle follow'd with such vigour on our side that in an hour they fell back and in an hour more they ran for it. We follow'd them close so that it concluded in a runaway retreat, some of the enemy into the town, the rest over St Charles River. GENERAL MONTCALM WAS KILL'D BY MY GRAPE SHOTT FROM A LIGHT SIXPOUNDER, his second whose name I know not now, a Brigadier and several officers kill'd, the whole of their kill'd and wounded I verily believe exceeds 2000 though that number is a French report. This happened the 13th instant since which I was very busy with my friend Mackellar in preparing to batter the town in breach, when the enemy surrender'd the 18th and I hoisted our Union flag on the walls of Quebec that same day. The town is much more batter'd than I imagined; 535 houses are burn'd down besides that, of the ricochet we have greatly shattered most of the rest. We are now putting the Garrison in a state to defend itself this winter."

Significance

A few men were aware of the importance of winning the French and Indian War. The Marquis de Montcalm clearly saw both its immediate and long range significance. He also knew that the outcome at Quebec would be a turning point. During the siege of Quebec he wrote:

Source: *The Marquis de Montcalm,* August 24, 1759 as quoted in Barney, Flowler, *The Adirondack Album,* Volume Two, New York, 1980, p. 29.

"M. Wolfe, if he understands his trade, will take to beat and ruin me if we meet in fight.

If he beats me here, France has lost America utterly: yes, and one's only conclusion is, in ten years farther, America will be in revolt against England!"

Robert Rogers, the Ranger, realized more than French statesmen, just what they had lost.

Source: Journals of Major Robert Rogers, *op cit,*. p. 142.

"Thus, at length, at the end of the fifth campaign, Montreal and the whole country of Canada was given up, and became subject to the King of Great Britain; a conquest perhaps of the greatest importance that is to be met with in the British annals, whether we consider the prodigious extent of country we are hereby made masters of, the vast addition it must make to trade and navigation, or the security it must afford to the northern provinces of America, particularly those flourishing ones of New England and New York, the irretrievable loss France sustains hereby, and the importance it must give the British crown among the several states of Europe: all this, I say, duly considered, will perhaps in its consequences render the year 1760 more glorious than any preceding.

And to this acquisition had we during the late war either by conquest or treaty added the fertile and extensive country of Louisiana, we should have been possessed of perhaps the most valuable territory upon the face of the globe, attended with more real advantages than the so much boasted mines of Mexico and Peru."

Conclusion

by
Mary Alice Burke Robinson

Part of the reason for the new taxes laid on the colonies by Britain was the cost of establishing forts along the frontier during the French and Indian War. Looked at from this point, Parliament was not making unreasonable or capricious demands on a prosperous colony. But the colonists saw these taxes as an imposition by a far-off government. The colonists were thinking of themselves more and more, not as British subjects, but as a new phenonemon. They were thinking of themselves as Americans, independent of restrictions and impositions.

When the threat of France was removed, the colonists no longer looked for support from Britian. They turned their former animosity toward France into a new spirit of independence. Spurred on by the success of the French and Indian War, the Americans soon became dissatisfied with their position in the British empire.

Just thirteen years later, the colonies demanded their independence. Many who fought in the French and Indian War (both Regulars and Provincials, i.e., both British and Americans) would soon be fighting on opposing sides.

The American soldiers who were veterans of the French and Indian War were far from being the green, unseasoned soldiers portrayed in popular histories. They understood guerrilla warfare. They were fighting on their own American soil with a very real stake in the future of America.

It has been said that if the British had used *Robert Rogers' Manual*, a handbook for guerrilla warfare, the British might not have lost this rich and vast land.

Glossary

Batteau - a type of boat used by the voyageurs (plural, *batteaux*)

Breastwork - a defensive work, usually chest high

Diaspora - the scattering of a people

Frigate - a fast naval vessel

Hogshead - a large cask, usually for holding liquid

Ononthio - an Indian word meaning chief

Portage - the carrying of canoes from one body of water to another

Redoubt - a small fort, usually completely enclosed

Schooner - various types of sailing vessels, with foremast and mainmast

Seigneurial system - a system of land holding used in New France

Siege - a systematic and often prolonged attack on a fortification

Skirling - emitting a high, shrill tone (from a bagpipe)

Suggested Further Reading

Note: Books cited at the beginning of each excerpt are also recommended for further reading.

Anderson, Fred, *A People's Army: Massachusetts Soldiers and Society in the Seven Years' War*. Chapel Hill: Published for The Institute of Early American History and Culture, Williamsburg, Virginia, by the University of North Carolina Press, 1984.

Bird, Harrison, *Battle for a Continent*. New York: Oxford University Press, 1965.

Carter, Alden R., *The Colonial Wars: Clashes in the Wilderness*. New York: Franklin Watts, 1992.

Chidsey, Donald Barr, *The French and Indian War: An Informal History*. New York, Crown Publishers, 1969.

Cooper, James Fenimore, *The Leatherstocking Tales: Volumes I, II; The Deerslayer, The Last of the Mohicans, The Pathfinder*. New York, The Library of America, 1985.

Demos, John, *The Unredeemed Captive: A Family Story from Early America*. New York, Alfred A. Knopf, 1994.

Edmonds, Walter D., *The Matchlock Gun*. New York, G. P. Putnam's Sons. 1989.

Marrin, Albert, *Struggle for a Continent: The French & Indian Wars 1690-1760*. New York: Atheneum, 1987.

Morton, Desmond, *New France and War*. Toronto, Grolier, Ltd. 1983.

North American Review, *The Bulletin of The Fort Ticonderoga Museum*, Volume IX, Summer 1954, Number 5.

Roberts, Kenneth, *Northwest Passage*. New York, Doubleday, 1936.

About the Editor

Mary Alice Burke Robinson holds bachelor's and master's degrees from State University of New York, Potsdam, New York. She taught in public schools on Long Island and northern New York, and was an adjunct professor for SUNY, Potsdam, teaching graduate level courses in curriculum and methods. Her professional writings include multidisciplinary units of study. She has long been a proponent of the use of primary source material in the classroom. She is currently an educational consultant, a Great Books discussion leader, and a genealogist.

Mrs. Robinson found this book of particular fascination because she makes her summer home on the St. Lawrence River, and is within a day's journey of Ticonderoga, Crown Point, Montreal and other major sites of the French and Indian War.

She and her husband, Dr. Eugene Westover Robinson, spend winters in Southern Arizona. Their four daughters live with their families in Watertown, Syracuse, and Ithaca, New York.